MW01247452

Would You Rather?
Easter Edition

Kiddley Press

WELCOME TO
"WOULD YOU RATHER?" EASTER EDITION

RULES OF THE GAME:

- SIT ACROSS FROM YOUR OPPONENT AND FACE THEM HEAD ON MAKING EYE CONTACT.

- FLIP A COIN, WHOEVER GUESSES CORRECTLY BECOMES "PLAYER 1" AND STARTS FIRST.

- PLAYER 1 READS THE FIRST "WOULD YOU RATHER" QUESTIONS ALOUD AND PLAYER 2 PICKS AN ANSWER.

- PLAYER 2 HAS TO EXPLAIN WHY THEY CHOOSE THEIR ANSWER.

- IF "PLAYER 2" LAUGHS THEN "PLAYER 1" GETS A LAUGH POINT!

- YOU ARE ALLOWED TO MAKE FUNNY FACES AND SOUND EFFECTS TO CRACK YOUR OPPONENT UP.

- NOTE: IT NEEDS TO BE AN AUDIBLE LAUGH - MEANING THERE HAS TO BE A SOUND OR A SMILE WHERE YOU CAN SEE THE OPPONENTS TEETH. ANYTHING ELSE DOESN'T COUNT.

- TAKE TURNS TO GO BACK AND FORTH AND AFTER EACH ROUND MARK YOUR TOTAL LAUGH POINTS.

- WHOEVER GETS THE MOST LAUGH POINTS IS CROWNED THE OFFICIAL "EASTER LAUGH CHAMPION!"

- IF THERE IS A TIE, FINISH WITH A TIE-BREAKER ROUND WHERE THE WINNER TAKES ALL!

DON'T FORGET TO HAVE FUN AND BE WACKY!

PLEASE REMEMBER THAT THE SCENARIOS DESCRIBED IN THIS BOOK ARE SOLELY FOR FUN AND GAMES. **DO NOT** ATTEMPT ANY OF THE CRAZY SCENARIOS LISTED!

ROUND
1

PLAYER

WOULD YOU RATHER BE COMPLETELY BALD LIKE AN EGG OR COVERED ALL OVER WITH HAIR LIKE A BUNNY?

WOULD YOU RATHER YOUR NAME BE CHANGED TO BOW THE BOUNCING BUNNY OR TO EL THE EXCITED EGG?

LAUGH POINT ___/2

 DON'T FORGET TO EXPLAIN YOUR ANSWERS

PLAYER 2

WOULD YOU RATHER BE MADE ENTIRELY OF CHOCOLATE OR ENTIRELY OF JELLO?

WOULD YOU RATHER HAVE A PET PEEP THAT CAN SPEAK OR A MUTE GIANT BUNNY YOU CAN RIDE ON?

LAUGH POINT ___/2

  DON'T FORGET TO EXPLAIN YOUR ANSWERS

PLAYER 1

WOULD YOU RATHER FLY ON A PLANE
MADE OUT OF PIZZA OR A TRAIN
MADE OF CANDY?

WOULD YOU RATHER FIGHT A GIANT
EASTER BUNNY USING ONLY YOUR LEGS
OR A MINIATURE ELEPHANT USING ONLY
YOUR HEAD?

LAUGH POINT ___/2

DON'T FORGET TO EXPLAIN YOUR ANSWERS

PLAYER 2

WOULD YOU RATHER TURN YOUR MOM OR YOUR DAD INTO A GIANT CHOCOLATE BUNNY?

WOULD YOU RATHER HAVE BIG BUNNY RABBIT TEETH THAT CAN'T FIT IN YOUR MOUTH OR FREAKY RED EYES LIKE A WHITE RABBIT?

LAUGH POINT ___/2

DON'T FORGET TO EXPLAIN YOUR ANSWERS

ADD UP YOUR SCORES AND RECORD THEM BELOW!

PLAYER 1 _____ /4
ROUND TOTAL

PLAYER 2 _____ /4
ROUND TOTAL

ROUND CHAMPION

ROUND
2

PLAYER 1

WOULD YOU RATHER EAT A 3 YEAR OLD CHOCOLATE EGG OR A PACKET OF JELLY BEANS THAT HAS FLEAS?

WOULD YOU RATHER HOP AROUND ON ALL FOURS FOR A DAY OR STICK FEATHERS ALL OVER YOUR ARMS AND PRETEND TO FLY ALL DAY?

LAUGH POINT ___/2

  DON'T FORGET TO EXPLAIN YOUR ANSWERS

PLAYER 2

WOULD YOU RATHER BE A PART OF AN ARMY OF RABBITS THROWING SMARTIES OR AN ARMY OF EGGS USING THEMSELVES AS WEAPONS?

WOULD YOU RATHER BE AS TALL AS THE EASTER ELEPHANT OR AS SHORT AS AN EASTER MOUSE?

LAUGH POINT ___/2

  DON'T FORGET TO EXPLAIN YOUR ANSWERS

PLAYER

WOULD YOU RATHER TAKE A BATH IN ICE CREAM OR CUSTARD?

WOULD YOU RATHER START EVERYTHING YOU SAY WITH "CHEEP CHEEP" LIKE A CHICK OR UNCONTROLLABLY THUMP YOUR FOOT ON THE GROUND LIKE A BUNNY AT RANDOM TIMES?

LAUGH POINT ___/2

  DON'T FORGET TO EXPLAIN YOUR ANSWERS

PLAYER  2

WOULD YOU RATHER HAVE COLORFUL EASTER EGG PATTERNS ALL OVER YOUR SKIN OR HAVE A FLOWER AS A HEAD?

WOULD YOU RATHER KEEP YOUR EASTER CANDY AND LET AN EAGLE SWOOP DOWN AND TAKE THE EASTER BUNNY OR SAVE THE EASTER BUNNY BUT THE EAGLE TAKES ALL OF YOUR EASTER CANDY?

LAUGH POINT ___/2

DON'T FORGET TO EXPLAIN YOUR ANSWERS

ADD UP YOUR SCORES AND RECORD THEM BELOW!

PLAYER

_____ /4
ROUND TOTAL

PLAYER

_____ /4
ROUND TOTAL

ROUND CHAMPION

ROUND
3

PLAYER 1

WOULD YOU RATHER HAVE A NOSE LIKE A BUNNY RABBIT OR A SHARP BEAK LIKE A CHICKEN?

WOULD YOU RATHER HAVE A KEY THAT CAN OPEN ANY DOOR OR A IMMORTAL CHICKEN THAT LAYS CHOCOLATE EGGS?

LAUGH POINT ___/2

 DON'T FORGET TO EXPLAIN YOUR ANSWERS

PLAYER 2

WOULD YOU RATHER BE ABLE TO TALK TO BIRDS AND TWEET AT PEOPLE OR BE ABLE TO TALK TO DOGS AND BARK AT PEOPLE?

WOULD YOU RATHER ONLY HAVE 4 ARMS OR 4 LEGS?

LAUGH POINT ___/2

  DON'T FORGET TO EXPLAIN YOUR ANSWERS

PLAYER 1

WOULD YOU RATHER HAVE TWIZZLERS FOR HAIR OR MARSHMALLOWS FOR FEET?

WOULD YOU RATHER HAVE TO FART LOUDLY AFTER EVERY BITE OF FOOD YOU EAT OR HAVE TO BURP AFTER EVERY SIP OF A DRINK?

LAUGH POINT ___/2

DON'T FORGET TO EXPLAIN YOUR ANSWERS

19

PLAYER 2

WOULD YOU RATHER SWEAT TOFFEE SAUCE EVERY TIME YOU GET HOT OR CRY DRY RAISINS?

WOULD YOU RATHER DO AN EASTER EGG HUNT WITH A MERMAID AT THE BOTTOM OF THE OCEAN OR WITH THE YETI IN THE MOUNTAINS?

LAUGH POINT ___/2

  DON'T FORGET TO EXPLAIN YOUR ANSWERS

ADD UP YOUR SCORES AND RECORD THEM BELOW!

PLAYER 1

_____ /4
ROUND TOTAL

PLAYER 2

_____ /4
ROUND TOTAL

_____

ROUND CHAMPION

ROUND
4

PLAYER 1

WOULD YOU RATHER BE CONTINUALLY
TRIPPING OVER EVERYTHING
OR CONTINUALLY BUMPING INTO
EVERYTHING?

WOULD YOU RATHER TELL BAD JOKES
AND MAKE EVERYONE GROAN FOR
AN HOUR EVERY DAY OR LISTEN TO
SOMEONE TELLING BAD JOKES FOR
AN HOUR EVERY DAY?

LAUGH POINT ___/2

DON'T FORGET TO EXPLAIN YOUR ANSWERS

PLAYER 2

WOULD YOU RATHER GET ONE EASTER EGG THAT REGROWS ITSELF AFTER EACH BITE OR FIND THREE EASTER EGGS EVERYDAY?

WOULD YOU RATHER HAVE TO ANNOUNCE TO EVERYONE WHENEVER YOU NEED TO FART OR ALWAYS SPILL WHATEVER YOU EAT OR DRINK ON YOURSELF?

LAUGH POINT ___/2

DON'T FORGET TO EXPLAIN YOUR ANSWERS

PLAYER 1

WOULD YOU RATHER HAVE YOUR PARENTS THROW A TANTRUM IN PUBLIC OR HAVE UNCONTROLLABLE LAUGHTER WHENEVER YOU SHOULD BE QUIET?

WOULD YOU RATHER LIVE IN A BURROW WITH THE EASTER BUNNY AND HIS CRAZY FAMILY OR LIVE IN A TREE WITH AN OLD WISE OWL AND FLY ON HIS BACK EVERYDAY?

LAUGH POINT ___/2

DON'T FORGET TO EXPLAIN YOUR ANSWERS

PLAYER

WOULD YOU RATHER BEGIN EVERY
SENTENCE WITH "HEY DUMMY" OR
FINISH EVERY SENTENCE YOU SAY WITH
"...HA HA, I WAS JUST KIDDING."

WOULD YOU RATHER HAVE BRIGHT
GREEN HANDS OR A MINIATURE YELLOW
TONGUE?

LAUGH POINT ___/2

  DON'T FORGET TO EXPLAIN YOUR ANSWERS

ADD UP YOUR SCORES AND RECORD THEM BELOW!

PLAYER

_____ /4
ROUND TOTAL

PLAYER

_____ /4
ROUND TOTAL

ROUND CHAMPION

ROUND
5

PLAYER

WOULD YOU RATHER TAKE A RIDE ON A LARGE CAT MADE OUT OF MARSHMALLOWS OR ON A CHIMPANZEE MADE OUT OF GUMMY BEARS?

WOULD YOU RATHER HAVE EASTER FOR A WHOLE YEAR ONCE IN YOUR LIFE OR CELEBRATE EASTER ONCE EVERY 4 YEARS?

LAUGH POINT ___/2

 DON'T FORGET TO EXPLAIN YOUR ANSWERS

PLAYER 2

WOULD YOU RATHER HAVE YOUR BREATH SMELL LIKE A DEAD FISH OR HAVE YOUR LAUGH SOUND LIKE A LONG FART?

WOULD YOU RATHER WEAR FLOPPY BUNNY EARS OR NOSE PLUGS THAT STICK OUT FOR ONE WEEK SRIAGHT?

LAUGH POINT ___/2

DON'T FORGET TO EXPLAIN YOUR ANSWERS

PLAYER 1

WOULD YOU RATHER HAVE A WEIRDLY MASSIVE MOUTH OR FREAKISHLY SMALL EYES?

WOULD YOU RATHER BE ABLE TO FLY OR BE ABLE TO WALK UP WALLS AND ON CEILINGS?

LAUGH POINT ___/2

DON'T FORGET TO EXPLAIN YOUR ANSWERS

31

PLAYER

WOULD YOU RATHER GIVE UP SWEETS AND CANDY OR SAVORY SNACKS LIKE POTATO CHIPS?

WOULD YOU RATHER BE STUCK TO A STICKY BEAR COVERED IN CARAMEL OR BE STUCK UP TO YOUR NECK IN VANILLA PUDDING?

LAUGH POINT ___/2

DON'T FORGET TO EXPLAIN YOUR ANSWERS

ADD UP YOUR SCORES AND RECORD THEM BELOW!

PLAYER 1   _____ /4
ROUND TOTAL

PLAYER 2   _____ /4
ROUND TOTAL

ROUND CHAMPION

ROUND
6

PLAYER 1

WOULD YOU RATHER CHIRP LIKE A CRICKET IN THE EVENING OR WADDLE LIKE A DUCK ALL DAY?

WOULD YOU RATHER LAY CHOCOLATE EASTER EGGS EVERYDAY OR HAVE A BEAUTIFUL PEACOCK'S TAIL?

LAUGH POINT ___/2

DON'T FORGET TO EXPLAIN YOUR ANSWERS

PLAYER 2

WOULD YOU RATHER BE A FUNNY BUNNY OR A SMART ELF?

WOULD YOU RATHER ALWAYS HOP UP STAIRS TWO AT A TIME OR HAVE TO SIT ON THE FLOOR EVERY TIME YOU RIDE IN AN ELEVATOR?

LAUGH POINT ___/2

DON'T FORGET TO EXPLAIN YOUR ANSWERS

PLAYER

WOULD YOU RATHER FIGHT 100 BUNNY SIZED ELEPHANTS OR 1 ELEPHANT SIZED BUNNY?

WOULD YOU RATHER GET CAUGHT STEALING EGGS FROM THE EASTER BUNNY OR HAVE A NOSE THAT GROWS EVERY TIME YOU LIE LIKE PINOCCHIO?

LAUGH POINT ___/2

 DON'T FORGET TO EXPLAIN YOUR ANSWERS

PLAYER 2

WOULD YOU RATHER HAVE X-RAY VISION OR A SUPERNATURAL SENSE OF SMELL FOR YOUR EASTER EGG HUNT?

WOULD YOU RATHER HAVE A TALKING BUTT OR A LOUD WHISTLING NOSE?

LAUGH POINT ___/2

DON'T FORGET TO EXPLAIN YOUR ANSWERS

ADD UP YOUR SCORES AND RECORD THEM BELOW!

PLAYER

_____ /4
ROUND TOTAL

PLAYER

_____ /4
ROUND TOTAL

ROUND CHAMPION

ROUND
7

PLAYER 1

WOULD YOU RATHER FALL INTO A GOOEY COMPOST HEAP FILLED WITH BUGS OR SWIM IN A LAKE FULL OF LEECHES?

WOULD YOU RATHER HAVE A GROUP OF ANNOYING RABBITS FOLLOW YOU EVERYWHERE YOU GO OR YELL AT THE TOP OF YOUR LUNGS EVERY TIME SOMEONE SAYS YOUR NAME?

LAUGH POINT ___/2

DON'T FORGET TO EXPLAIN YOUR ANSWERS

PLAYER 2

WOULD YOU RATHER GET PAID FOR A JOB IN CANDY OR PAID IN CASH?

WOULD YOU RATHER BE RAISED BY BUNNIES OR RAISED BY MONKEYS?

LAUGH POINT ___/2

DON'T FORGET TO EXPLAIN YOUR ANSWERS

42

PLAYER 1

WOULD YOU RATHER EAT A PLATE OF DUST BUNNIES ON A WAFFLE OR 1 LIVE WORM DIPPED IN SHERBET?

WOULD YOU RATHER CALL EVERYONE THAT YOU MEET A "SILLY EGGGGGGG!" WHEN SAYING HELLO OR HAVE TO LAY FACE DOWN ON THE GROUND WHEN SOMEONE GREETS YOU?

LAUGH POINT ___/2

  DON'T FORGET TO EXPLAIN YOUR ANSWERS

PLAYER 2

WOULD YOU RATHER SMELL LIKE
A ROTTEN EGG AND NOT KNOW OR
ALWAYS SMELL ROTTEN EGG BUT
NO ONE ELSE CAN SMELL IT?

WOULD YOU RATHER HAVE A CAT
WITH A HUMAN FACE OR A DOG
WITH HUMAN HANDS AND FEET?

LAUGH POINT ___/2

DON'T FORGET TO EXPLAIN YOUR ANSWERS

ADD UP YOUR SCORES AND RECORD THEM BELOW!

PLAYER 1

___ /4
ROUND TOTAL

PLAYER 2

___ /4
ROUND TOTAL

___

ROUND CHAMPION

ROUND
8

PLAYER 1

WOULD YOU RATHER HAVE THE
EASTER BUNNY RULE THE WORLD OR
YOUR MOM RULE THE WORLD?

WOULD YOU RATHER SPEAK ONLY BUNNY
LANGUAGE AND NEED A TRANSLATOR
OR ONLY BE ABLE TO SPEAK WHEN
SOMEONE ASKS YOU A QUESTION?

LAUGH POINT ___/2

  DON'T FORGET TO EXPLAIN YOUR ANSWERS

PLAYER 2

WOULD YOU RATHER HAVE A BUNNY'S TAIL AS BIG AS YOUR HEAD OR BUNNY PAWS FOR HANDS?

WOULD YOU RATHER LIVE WITH A BORING CHICKEN IN A HOUSE MADE OF CANDY OR LIVE WITH YOUR FAVORITE CARTOON CHARACTER IN AN OLD RUN DOWN HUT?

LAUGH POINT ___/2

DON'T FORGET TO EXPLAIN YOUR ANSWERS

PLAYER

WOULD YOU RATHER WALK BACKWARD ALL THE TIME OR WALK ON YOUR HANDS EVERYWHERE?

WOULD YOU RATHER BE ABLE TO SHOOT CANDY OUT OF YOUR FINGERTIPS OR SNEEZE CHOCOLATE COVERED MARSHMALLOWS?

LAUGH POINT ___/2

 DON'T FORGET TO EXPLAIN YOUR ANSWERS

PLAYER

WOULD YOU RATHER HAVE TOE SIZED LEGS OR LEG SIZED TOES?

WOULD YOU RATHER EAT CHOCOLATE FLAVORED BUNNY POOP OR BUNNY POOP FLAVORED CHOCOLATE?

LAUGH POINT ___/2

  DON'T FORGET TO EXPLAIN YOUR ANSWERS

ADD UP YOUR SCORES AND RECORD THEM BELOW!

PLAYER

/4

ROUND TOTAL

PLAYER

/4

ROUND TOTAL

ROUND CHAMPION

ROUND
9

PLAYER

WOULD YOU RATHER PAINT AN EASTER EGG WITH YOUR ELBOWS OR YOUR KNEES?

WOULD YOU RATHER DO AN EASTER EGG HUNT USING ONLY YOUR TOES OR ONLY YOUR BUTT CHEEKS?

LAUGH POINT ___/2

 DON'T FORGET TO EXPLAIN YOUR ANSWERS

PLAYER ②

WOULD YOU RATHER UNCONTROLLABLY SPIT ON PEOPLE AT THE EASTER PARTY OR UNCONTROLLABLY GRAB THEIR CANDY AND EAT IT IN FRONT OF THEM?

WOULD YOU RATHER CLUCK LIKE A CHICKEN EVERY TIME YOU LAUGH OR BRAY LIKE A DONKEY EVERY TIME YOU LAUGH?

LAUGH POINT ___/2

  DON'T FORGET TO EXPLAIN YOUR ANSWERS

54

PLAYER 1

WOULD YOU RATHER HAVE THE
EASTER BUNNY AS YOUR BEST FRIEND
OR TURN YOUR BEST FRIEND INTO
THE EASTER BUNNY?

WOULD YOU RATHER GO ON AN
EASTER EGG HUNT WITH SHERLOCK
HOLMES OR GO ON AN EASTER
EGG HUNT WITH SPIDERMAN?

LAUGH POINT ___/2

DON'T FORGET TO EXPLAIN YOUR ANSWERS

PLAYER 2

WOULD YOU RATHER POOP CHOCOLATE EASTER EGGS OR THROW UP CANDY PEEPS WHENEVER YOU WANTED?

WOULD YOU RATHER GO DOWN A RABBIT HOLE WITH THE EASTER BUNNY TO HIS HIDDEN CANDY PALACE OR FLY WITH SANTA AND HIS REINDEERS IN AN OPEN SLEIGH?

LAUGH POINT ___/2

DON'T FORGET TO EXPLAIN YOUR ANSWERS

56

ADD UP YOUR SCORES AND RECORD THEM BELOW!

PLAYER

_____ /4
ROUND TOTAL

PLAYER

_____ /4
ROUND TOTAL

ROUND CHAMPION

ROUND
10

PLAYER 1

WOULD YOU RATHER TEAM UP WITH THE EASTER BUNNY OR A CRAZY CHOCOLATE EGG IN A RACE?

WOULD YOU RATHER LIVE WITHOUT CARTOONS FOR THE REST OF YOUR LIFE BUT HAVE UNLIMITED CANDY OR WATCH CARTOONS WHENEVER YOU WANT BUT NEVER EAT CANDY?

LAUGH POINT ___/2

DON'T FORGET TO EXPLAIN YOUR ANSWERS

PLAYER  2

WOULD YOU RATHER HAVE A SING OFF WITH ALICE IN WONDERLAND OR A DANCE OFF WITH THE WHITE RABBIT?

WOULD YOU RATHER WATCH ONLY BORING NEWS CHANNELS DURING THE HOLIDAYS OR ONLY SCARY HORROR MOVIES?

LAUGH POINT ___/2

  DON'T FORGET TO EXPLAIN YOUR ANSWERS

PLAYER

WOULD YOU RATHER BE AN 11 FOOT EASTER BUNNY OR A 3 INCH PEEP?

WOULD YOU RATHER EAT EVERYTHING AT EASTER DINNER WITH A HAIR CLIP OR WITH YOUR TOOTHBRUSH?

LAUGH POINT ___/2

  DON'T FORGET TO EXPLAIN YOUR ANSWERS

PLAYER ②

WOULD YOU RATHER NEVER BE ABLE TO EAT CANDY AGAIN OR NEVER SEE YOUR BEST FRIEND AGAIN?

WOULD YOU RATHER ALWAYS HAVE A BOOGER IN YOUR NOSE THAT MOVES WHEN YOU BREATHE OR HAVE FOOD STUCK BETWEEN YOUR FRONT TEETH?

LAUGH POINT ___/2

DON'T FORGET TO EXPLAIN YOUR ANSWERS

ADD UP YOUR SCORES AND RECORD THEM BELOW!

PLAYER _____ /4
ROUND TOTAL

PLAYER _____ /4
ROUND TOTAL

ROUND CHAMPION

ROUND
11

PLAYER 1

WOULD YOU RATHER HAVE TO WEAR YOUR SHIRT BACKWARD OR YOUR PANTS INSIDE OUT ON EASTER DAY?

WOULD YOU RATHER FIND NO EASTER EGGS BUT MEET THE EASTER BUNNY OR FIND EASTER EGGS BUT NEVER MEET THE EASTER BUNNY?

LAUGH POINT ___/2

 DON'T FORGET TO EXPLAIN YOUR ANSWERS

PLAYER 2

WOULD YOU RATHER EAT ONLY CANDY FOR A YEAR OR EAT ONLY PIZZA FOR A YEAR?

WOULD YOU RATHER GO TO THE CENTRE OF THE EARTH WITH THE EASTER BUNNY OR GO TO THE MOON WITH A ROCKETSHIP ALONE?

LAUGH POINT ___/2

DON'T FORGET TO EXPLAIN YOUR ANSWERS

PLAYER 1

WOULD YOU RATHER BE THE FUNNIEST PERSON OR THE SMARTEST PERSON ON EASTER?

WOULD YOU RATHER ALWAYS FART RAINBOWS THAT STINK BADLY OR ALWAYS FART SUPER LOUDLY?

LAUGH POINT ___/2

  DON'T FORGET TO EXPLAIN YOUR ANSWERS

PLAYER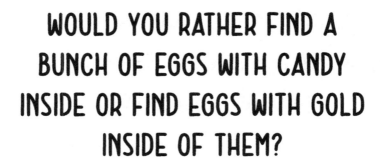

WOULD YOU RATHER FIND A BUNCH OF EGGS WITH CANDY INSIDE OR FIND EGGS WITH GOLD INSIDE OF THEM?

WOULD YOU RATHER DO AN UNPREPARED SPEECH IN FRONT OF 15 000 PEOPLE OR KISS A SLIMY FROG?

LAUGH POINT ___/2

DON'T FORGET TO EXPLAIN YOUR ANSWERS

ADD UP YOUR SCORES AND RECORD THEM BELOW!

PLAYER

/4
_____
ROUND TOTAL

PLAYER

/4
_____
ROUND TOTAL

ROUND CHAMPION

ROUND
12

PLAYER 1

WOULD YOU RATHER BE THE UGLIEST PERSON IN THE WORLD OR THE SMELLIEST PERSON IN THE WORLD?

WOULD YOU RATHER HAVE TO FLOSS THE EASTER BUNNIES TEETH EVERYDAY OR HELP THE TOOTH FAIRY CARRY ALL THE KIDS' TEETH EVERYDAY?

LAUGH POINT ___/2

  DON'T FORGET TO EXPLAIN YOUR ANSWERS

PLAYER 2

WOULD YOU RATHER KISS AN ANGRY CROCODILE'S TONGUE OR GET BITTEN BY A CRAZY KOALA BEAR?

WOULD YOU RATHER BE SMACKED IN THE FACE WITH AN EASTER BASKET OR BE FARTED ON BY A STINKY CHICKEN?

LAUGH POINT ___/2

DON'T FORGET TO EXPLAIN YOUR ANSWERS

PLAYER  1

WOULD YOU RATHER GO THROUGH LIFE WITH ONLY ONE NOSTRIL OR LIVE WITH ONLY ONE EAR?

WOULD YOU RATHER POOP IN THE TOILET AT THE EASTER PARTY KNOWING THAT YOU'LL CLOG IT OR WOULD YOU LET EVERYONE KNOW THAT YOU WILL POOP IN THE BUSHES OUTSIDE?

LAUGH POINT ___/2

 DON'T FORGET TO EXPLAIN YOUR ANSWERS

PLAYER 2

WOULD YOU RATHER GO TO EASTER DINNER COMPLETELY NAKED OR HAVE EVERYONE BE NAKED AT EASTER DINNER EXCEPT YOU?

WOULD YOU RATHER LIVE WITH A STINKY SKUNK SMELL ON ALL OF YOUR CLOTHES OR LIVE WITH COW DUNG AND UNCOMFY PEBBLES IN YOUR SHOES?

LAUGH POINT ___/2

  DON'T FORGET TO EXPLAIN YOUR ANSWERS

ADD UP YOUR SCORES AND RECORD THEM BELOW!

PLAYER

/4

ROUND TOTAL

PLAYER

/4

ROUND TOTAL

_____

ROUND CHAMPION

ROUND
13

PLAYER

WOULD YOU RATHER PUT A HYPERACTIVE HAMSTER IN YOUR PANTS OR LET A HAIRY CENTIPEDE CRAWL ON YOUR FACE?

WOULD YOU RATHER GIVE ALL OF YOUR EASTER CANDY TO YOUR LEAST FAVORITE PERSON AND HAVE NONE ON EASTER OR HAVE ALL THE CANDY YOU WANT ON EASTER BUT SPEND THE REST OF THE YEAR WITH NO CANDY?

LAUGH POINT ___/2

  DON'T FORGET TO EXPLAIN YOUR ANSWERS

PLAYER 2

WOULD YOU RATHER HAVE A SICK
BABY VOMIT ON YOU OR WOULD
YOU RATHER BE SICK AND VOMIT
ON A BABY?

WOULD YOU RATHER HAVE A TEA PARTY
WITH THE MAD HATTER AND HAVE
UNCONTROLLABLE HICCUPS OR A DINNER
PARTY WITH THE SMURFS AND BURP
EVERY 5 SECONDS?

LAUGH POINT ___/2

DON'T FORGET TO EXPLAIN YOUR ANSWERS

PLAYER 1

WOULD YOU RATHER POOP EVERY TIME YOU LAUGH OR PEE EVERY TIME YOU CRY?

WOULD YOU RATHER HAVE A PET BUNNY RABBIT THAT POOPS ON YOUR FEET ALL DAY OR A BABY CHICK THAT WAKES YOU UP AND PECKS YOU IN YOUR SLEEP?

LAUGH POINT ___/2

DON'T FORGET TO EXPLAIN YOUR ANSWERS

PLAYER 2

WOULD YOU RATHER STAY CLEAN FOREVER AND NEVER HAVE TO SHOWER AGAIN OR ALWAYS HAVE SPARKLY TEETH AND NEVER HAVE TO BRUSH YOUR TEETH EVER AGAIN?

WOULD YOU RATHER TRIP AND FLY ACROSS THE FLOOR WITH YOUR FAVORITE DESSERT IN HAND OR EAT TOO MUCH AND VOMIT ON THE TABLE AT EASTER DINNER?

LAUGH POINT ___/2

DON'T FORGET TO EXPLAIN YOUR ANSWERS

ADD UP YOUR SCORES AND RECORD THEM BELOW!

PLAYER

_____ /4
ROUND TOTAL

PLAYER

_____ /4
ROUND TOTAL

ROUND CHAMPION

THE END.... ALMOST!

WE HOPE YOU LIKED THIS BOOK AND THAT IT GOT PLENTY OF SMILES AND CHUCKLES OUT OF YOUR LITTLE ONES THIS EASTER!

HERE'S SOMETHING THAT IS NOT A JOKE, REVIEWS – THEY CAN MAKE OR BREAK AN AUTHOR'S CAREER.

AS A SMALL INDEPENDENT AUTHOR WITH A TINY BUDGET, I RELY ON READERS, LIKE YOU, TO LEAVE REVIEWS ON AMAZON.

EVEN IF IT'S JUST A SENTENCE OR TWO.

SO IF YOU ENJOYED THIS BOOK PLEASE LEAVE ME A BRIEF REVIEW.

I VERY MUCH APPRECIATE EVERY REVIEW THAT I RECEIVE AND IT TRULY MAKES A DIFFERENCE!

THANK YOU FOR PURCHASING THIS BOOK AND READING ALL THE WAY TO THE END.

HOPPY EASTER!

Made in the USA
Monee, IL
25 March 2022

93562106R00050